About The Author

Laura Davis is a British-born European poet who currently lives in Kampala, Uganda.

Her poems have appeared in *Seen as Read* (Kingston University Press, 2020), *Live Canon Anthology* 2020, *Writers Kingston, Ink Sweat and Tears and in the Penteract Anthology 2022* (forthcoming). This is her first collection.

Laura tweets @LaDaBel and can also be found on Instagram at @lauradavis1709.

Found & Lost

&

Laura Davis

KU
PRESS

Typeset in Timeless, Courier ST, and Microsoft PhagsPa.
Photographs and artwork © Laura Davis, 2022

Editorial and Design by Kingston University MA Publishing Students:
Sophie Boddington
Zoe Bott
Miranda González Farrington
Arwa Nadeem
Vanshika Parmar

KINGSTON UNIVERSITY PRESS
Kingston University
Penrhyn Road
Kingston-upon-Thames
KT1 2EE

Foreword

I am a European born and raised British in the UK, an immigrant to Belgium and a white expatriate living in Kinshasa, Jerusalem and Kampala, someone who lives between languages in a mixed-language family and where many words around me, in the places where I live, escape my grasp.

Most of these poems were written during the period that included Brexit and the Covid pandemic.

During this time, listening to some of the classic literary works in English became a refuge, and the main source of the found text in many of these poems. *Illustrations and Interruptions* draws on aurally found texts of audiobook performances of Victorian classics, with some responses inspired by twentieth century abstract art, and *Evitan on Ikenild Street* is a poem play using text found in Thomas Hardy's *The Return of the Native.*

The poems in *Desert Water Wind* respond to some of the people and places I have met, seen and visited over the past years.

Park Walks started in pre-pandemic Jerusalem, as a reflection on how parks are spaces used by people of all backgrounds – although not equally. During the pandemic, when I was 'evacuated' with my children from Kampala to Brussels, I, like other flat-livers, came to rely on local parks as (limited) spaces for movement. At the same time, Black Lives Matter reminded us of how these apparently open spaces celebrate European imperialism and the repression of so many people globally.

Vent is three Mathews Corpus that use words spelt the same in English and in French and with different meanings.

Back in Kampala, the Northern powers continued to look away from the continent. In the run-up to the elections in January 2021, police broke up opposition protests in major towns in Uganda. The sequence *November* uses found text from newspaper reports from the *Daily Monitor* of the demonstrations in Uganda's capital during 18-20 November 2020, in which more than 50 people died. Hundreds of people – there is no confirmed total – have disappeared during the electoral process.

The collection closes with a series of visual poems, *H, darkly.*

Kampala, January 2022

Contents

I. Illustrations and Interruptions

**Listening to *The Return of the Native*
while waiting for the vaccine**

After Kazimir Malevich,
Black and White,
Suprematist Composition 1915

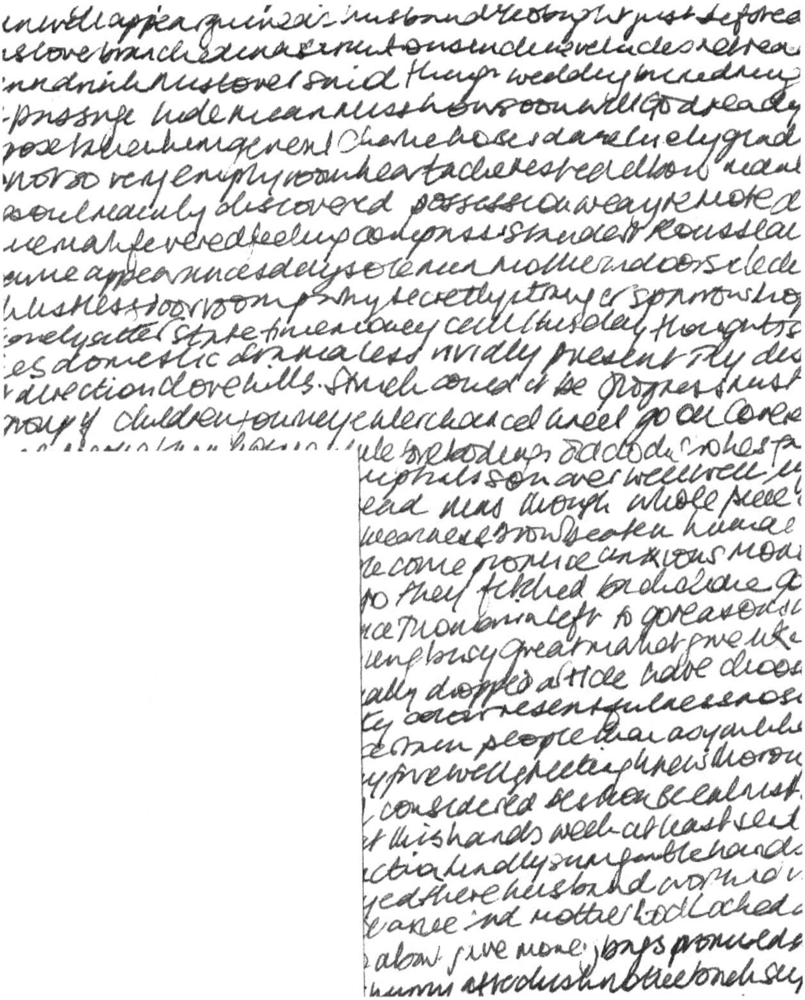

Bleak House
After Raymond Haims, *Sans Titre 1950-1954*

After RAYMOND HAINS
Sans titre 1950-54

Middlemarch I

15

The Way We Live Now I

The Way We Live Now II

The Way We Live Now SN474 11-June-2021

medipal
INTERNATIONAL HOSPITAL
Life is Precious

MEDIPAL INTERNATIONAL HOSPITAL
Plot 1A Lower Kololo Terrace, Kampala, Contact +2564177...
P.O. Box 26585 Kampala, Uganda, Email: corona@medipal.ug

COVID-19 TEST RESULTS

Test Method: PCR

Result No.:

District: Kampala

Public Health Passenger Locator Form

HEALTH, FOOD CHAIN SAFETY
AND ENVIRONMENT

Thank you for helping us protect your health

brussels airlines
STAR ALLIANCE MEMBER

ENGER NAME: DAVIS / LAURA
KET NUMBER: 0823855503407
ent Flyer No.: LH-XXXXXXXXXXX193 LH
-in Sequence No.: 034

BOARDING PASS

EBBE (EBB)	To BRUSSELS (BRU)	Flight No. SN 474
N21	Departure 23:55	Class of Travel ECONOMY
	Boarding Time 23:25	Seat 29D

Baggage drop-off at the airport latest 90 minutes before scheduled time of flight departure

BAGGAGE ... Business Class: 2 pieces (16kg total), Premium Economy and Economy class: 1 piece (max 8 kg).
... size per piece: 55x40x23cm. W... ...elling with another airline, contact them for carry-on information.
-ROP-OFF ... ...ossible until 40 minutes (*) before departure for ...ights within Europe and until 70 minutes (*) before departure
... for flights to and from Africa/USA and Canada. (*) Unless otherwise indicated above.

GOODS ... are not allowed in either carry-on luggage or in checked luggage. More information on www.brusselsairlines.com

The Way We Live Now III

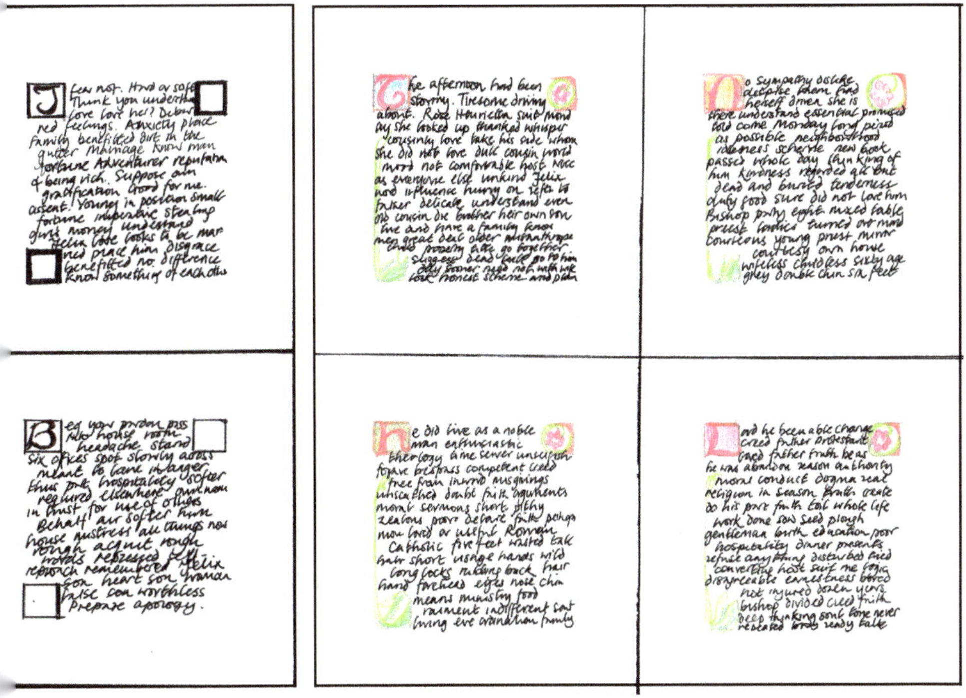
J
fear not. Hard or soft
Think you understand
love love her? Debar
red feelings. Anxiety place
family benefitted dirt in the
gutter marriage know man
fortune Adventurer reputation
of being rich. Suppose own
gratification Good for me.
assent. Young in position small
fortune sterling
girls money understand
Felix love looks to be mar
ried place him disgrace
benefitted no difference
know something of each other
B
eg your pardon pass
into house room
headache stand
six offices spot slowly across
meant to lane danger
thus hospitality softer
required elsewhere
in trust for use of others
Behalf air softer him
house mistress all things now
rough acquit rough
words repressed
reproach remembered Felix
son heart son woman
false worthless
Prepare apology.
T
he afternoon had been
stormy. Tiresome driving
about. Rose Henrietta
she looked up thanked whisper
cousinly love take his side whom
she did not love dull cousin
not comfortable host
as everyone else unkind Felix
influence hurry on
delicate understand even
old cousin die brother heir own son
live and have a family
men great deal older misanthrope
property go together
suggest dead go to him
day sooner need not
look honest scheme and plan
N
o sympathy dislike
despise whom find
herself driven she is
there understand essential promised
told come Monday
as possible neighbourhood
idleness scheme new book
passed whole day thinking of
him kindness regarded all but
dead and buried tenderness
duty good sure did not love him
Bishop party eight mixed table
priest turned
courteous young priest
courtesy own house
wifeless childless sixty age
grey double chin six feet
H
e did live as a noble
man enthusiastic
theology time server unselfish
competent creed
free from inward misgivings
unscathed doubt faith arguments
moral sermons short pithy
zealous before faith perhaps
more loved or useful Roman
Catholic five feet wasted talk
hair short usage hands wild
long locks rubbing back hair
hand forehead eyes nose chin
means ministry food
raiment indifferent sort
living eve ordination family
H
ad he been able change
creed father protestant
creed father truth bear
he was abandon reason authority
moral conduct dogma zeal
religion in season truth create
do his part faith toil whole life
work done sow seed plough
gentleman birth education poor
hospitality dinner presents
refuse anything disturbed tried
converting host
disagreeable earnestness bored
not injured dozen years
bishop divided creed faith
deep thinking soul gone never
repeated words ready talk

Vanity Fair

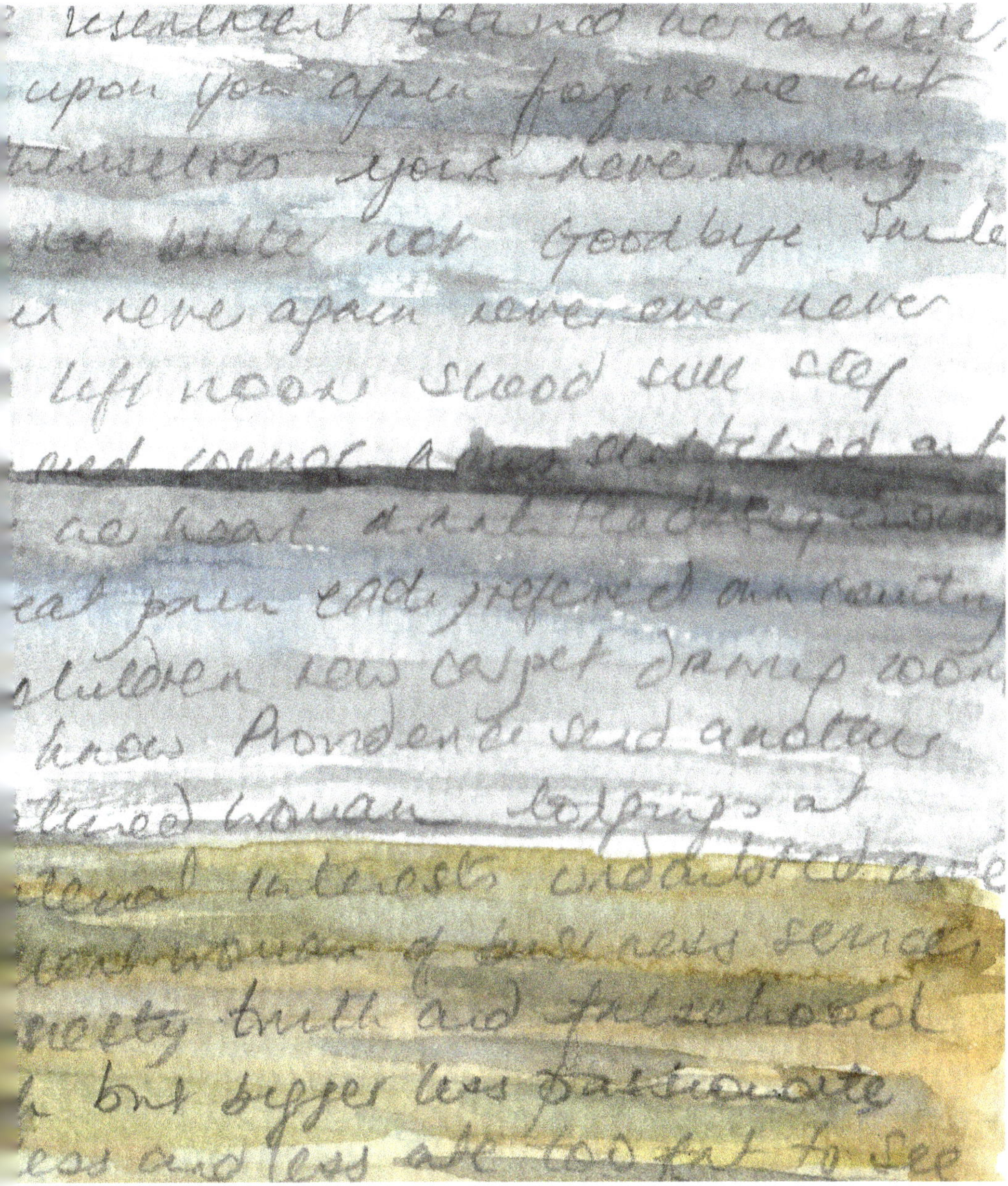

Hard Times

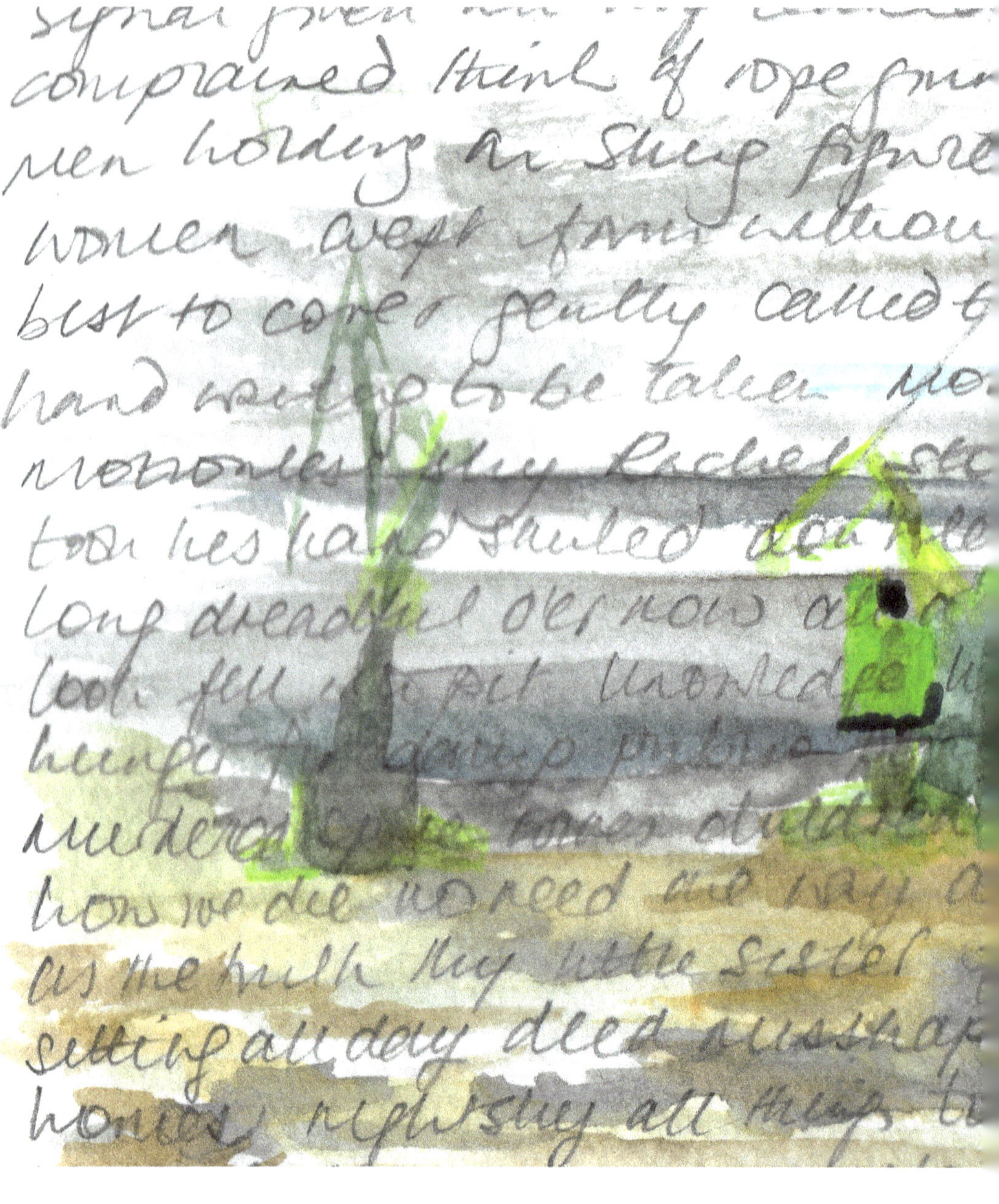

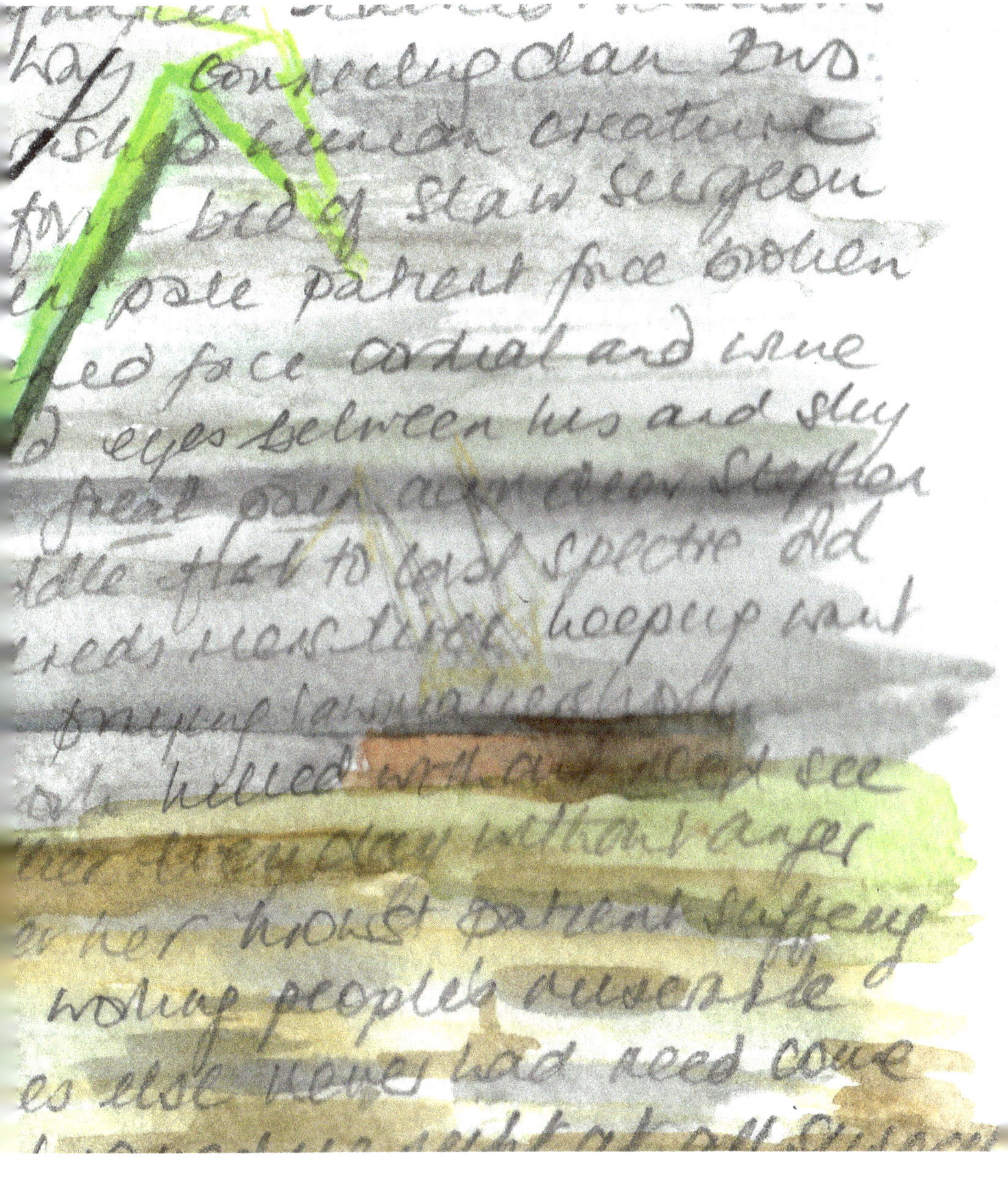

A Tale of Two Cities

II. Desert Water Wind

Reel

Do not open! The only words I can read
on the gas mask box,
next to the iron, above the coats,
never seen used life before, only on film.
Now, as I turn in the reel,

I see the crack in the wall of my first home
from those newsreel-bombs thirty years before
on the city that nearly fell in on itself -
not the Birmingham bombs on my birthday (I never saw them)
there were no bunkers then but mutterings about neighbours,
you know, *them*, sliding glances from upstairs rooms
years later, still keeping an eye out, you know.

Turn back to this flat. Its safe room's my study,
safe because it's under external stairs.
If They come for real we will hunker down and open the boxes.
Will google translate work for the instructions?

Around again: Four people, eight cases
baggage swung onto the check-in belt
pay the excess, give up our visas
leave the desert for tropical green
two steps over from where we were before before.
The rhythm changes and I remember these steps.
A flash of cloth, a turn of phrase
the smell of charcoal held in equatorial heat.

Turn again and now in cold rain
Ambiorix the Gaul faces down Caesar
before art nouveau mansions built from rubber
ivory and copper, no coltan then,
down the small street, out to Maelbeek station
(a gas mask's no good if the metro's blown out)
I turn slightly to pass through the turnstile
step into the carriage and sway on my way.

Desert

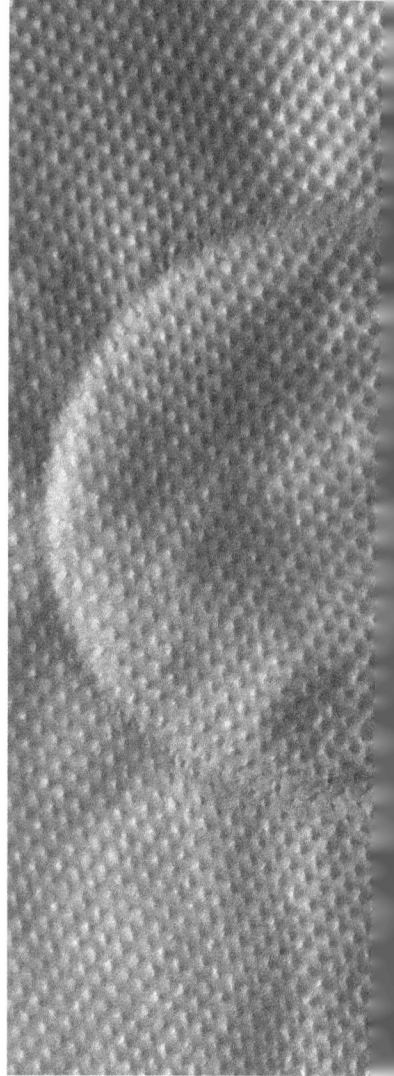

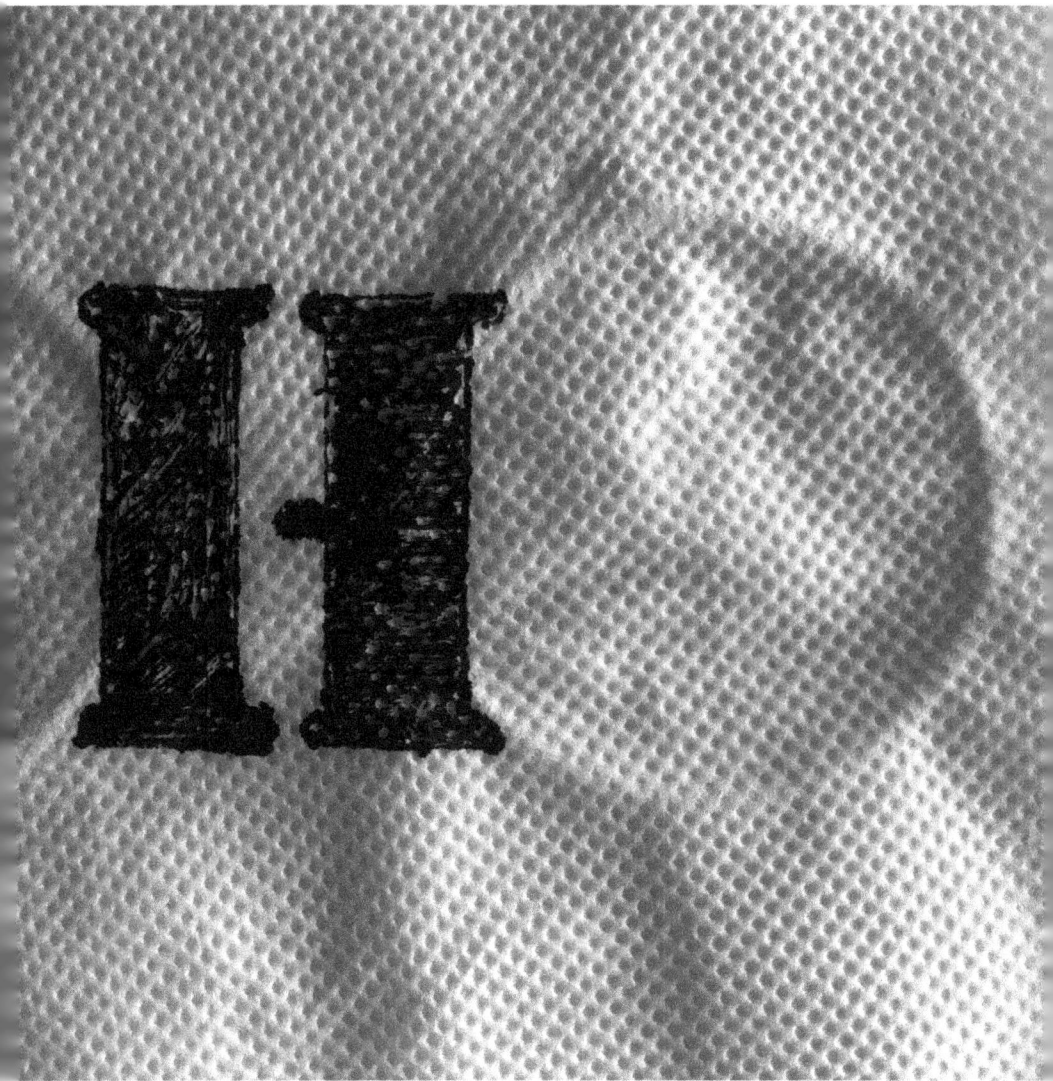

Wadi Qelt

At the spring, the desert is lime green.
I follow the stream encased in stone
two thousand years hewn,
a leafbound slash along the wadi wall.
Hillsides rise all around, pebbledash undulating
along and across the depths of the gorge.
I look to the reeds and they reground me.

The clink of bells spirals down,
draws my gaze up to seek out the sheep
pinched onto outcrops, their long ears,
smooth noses and ragged fleeces
merging with planes and the ledges of the cliff.
I think I glimpse a shepherd higher up
but it's a plastic bag caught in a thorn bush.

The path descends to smooth rock strata,
then to swirled boulders,
the wake of a long-dry torrent
piled closer and closer
then I'm crawling through a tunnel
of reeds, thicker and stronger than my forearm,
emerging to a column of seedheads nodding down at me.

At midday I stop to perch on a broad overhang
watching the waves of rock strata and grit
shift and curve, settle and shift before my eyes,
motion I understand as I accept I am as in a boat
and the greys, and ochres, and greens and browns will swell
and shift and carry me along so long as I do not resist
and my breath slows to the rhythm of the rock.

The path slopes forward. A fox lopes away
towards the plain in far-off blue-green haze
beyond where the aqueduct slices the gorge
where from its block-shade three forms emerge,
burdened, black-swathed, toiling up the path
that has borne people and water for thousands of years.
Are they Bedouin or walkers? Settlers or monks? Binoculars don't help.

They plod out of sight. An eagle passes high overhead
a snapped blink in the sunlight.
My rock is between their path and the drop
I stand and brush lunch crumbs from my bright hiking kit
in the hope (out of habit) that I will be seen-oveseen-overlooked.
My phone in my hand,
the desert continues as I hold my breath.

Eyes down, they round the bend
hunched under huge backpacks
- only small logos place them in our time -
nuns chanting their pace, steady, steadfastly.
The first raises her head and nods
as they skirt the rock
and carry their prayers on out of sight.

At the pool, I lie on fine grass and bright star flowers
by cool water so clear the fish seem to fly through air
away from my heat-swollen hands
refracted puffy and dull against shiny taut pebbles.

A lone cloud smudges the desert sun.
Its shadow chills me. Then it is gone.

Sundowner
Odysseus at the Dead Sea

Sky flares green as the sun falls back
behind the mountain range
flat sea convulses pink and violet,
water that never lets you sink.

    Their eyes hard over wine.
    We can't all be clever like you!
    nearly laughed
    hangs on in the hall, follows me still.

    That trick with the horse.
    They loved it, of course.
    Until they didn't and it couldn't sit right
    with the nevereverending drone of who killed whom.
    Not much of an inspiration for the lads now is it?

The water deepens -
not the sludge-brown of blood through soil,
but crimson holding the last stabs of yellow light,
dry-heavings of the bravest men.

Ah, but Achilles, now there's a proper hero.
Action, not fancy schemes. Good example for the men.
Fighting's easier, mind, when your ma
arrow-proofed you at birth, has the right ears.

The glory of his death
pointless for Troy and Helen, even Patroclus and Hector.
Glittering loss as a win
brave, not clever.

The sea fights the dark although it knows
the sun will rise again tomorrow,
heat the deadwater that poisons the land and chars my skin.

Green Orange

Grazing sheep on a hillside
steep cliff, lime over sea
She waves, I turn, gulls
dive-bomb chip-eaters
paper cones equations with π
whipped cream milk cartons
open and closed and in-between.

Sour, stings my palette
cadmium yellow, veridian hue
alizarine crimson
sandstone desert moon
sharp light citrus tang at dusk
white flowers in glossy green leaves.

Sous la pluie,
j'ai fait la crêpe

pancakes
lean flat
last fat
flipping hot
forty desert days
I bake in the rain
drizzle lemon
ash dissolves

Note: *faire la crêpe*, literally, in French, 'to make a pancake', means to bake yourself sunbathing, but it was raining on Shrove Tuesday.

Midsummer

Faraway windows across the valley
flash our setting sun back across minefields

living rooms blazing beyond no man's land -
beacons broadcasting mountain positions.

Mynahs, bulbuls, sparrows and soot-clad jays
lunge and dart after invisible prey

rising as green spears pierce charred earth
while hoopoes bore down below.

The sun sets too early here. But tonight
we will go out through the checkpoint

and in Nadia's garden past the wall, we will dance,
grapevine garlands in our hair

beneath the midsummer moon.

Trade Winds

The builders are drilling again.
I walk to the café with kumquat trees
where the barista suggests something new.
Voices ebb around me, some I understand.
We lone regulars nod, half-greet
retreat to our smartphones.

Here I can pass and almost fit in.
Out in the open, my nerves tighten
for "Wait! Stop! You there!"
and the boys with guns, the girl on the bike,
the women with prams, the man with the dog
will turn and stare at the outsider
revealed and reviled, and chase me back to

my kind, who migrate like birds obeying
unknown seasons, a pattern
of postings following modern trade winds
cuckoo-roosting in nests ornate
with objects gathered in foreign parts,
by keepsakes from homes now half-remembered.

I will move on when the wind changes.
Maybe to that place I still call home,
my bags heavier, another space
between my roots and me.

I think I can still play the part -
carefully, mind, for fear
the perennial imposter is unmasked.

On Lake Victoria

Storm clouds hang out over the island, heavy
rain has cooled the thermals and killed the wind. We
drift, not sail, towards open water, rocking
into the soft swell.

Thunder rages, but these are empty threats – it's
grounded on the southerly hills, the lightening
towed behind. The clouds soften, lift and disperse
brightening the sky.

Dead ahead the wind rises. Close-hauled, we skim
cresting waves, surf sluicing our bows, our bodies
over water, fighting the sail, the windpower
forcing up our speed.

Egrets pass us, flowing around our sails. Kites
hover over kingfishers diving straight down.
Cormorants dip into our wake as we glide
past as if unseen.

You fly past, adrenaline whoops the only
noise save whooshing fibreglass over water,
orange lifevest stark in the sun. Your capped head
turns to me: thumbs up.

All the scenes I played out before – electric
storms, exhaustion, capsizing- I missed just one
possibility: of a great day's sailing
out on Nyanza.

Dying Below
Lake Victoria

Sunrise, and in silhouette
fishermen in dugouts row
through you to their sunken nets
while you are dying below.

You make weather: clouds, and rain
falling where trees used to grow,
holding run-off that now drains
into you, dying below.

Kingfishers and eagles dive,
dragonflies and stilts skim low
swallow their prey still alive
unaware that you are dying below.

Nighttime. Fireflies rise and shine,
silver from the harvest moon
hides how we've so little time
to stop you dying below.

Night Swim

My body rises

    unfurls

        each part distances

            finds the right height

    cold   steals   up my hair

      cradles   my   scalp

        rocks my head
        sky ward

    light drowns at the horizon
    cloud swamps moon and stars

    I shrink to a sandgrain

    in slate-water
breeze-washed knees breasts face
    waves rake the shore
    salt purls my ears

    laughter surfs from the beach
    voices reel me in
    toes ground in the sand

        I skim the foam, regaining

Zandwaterspiegel

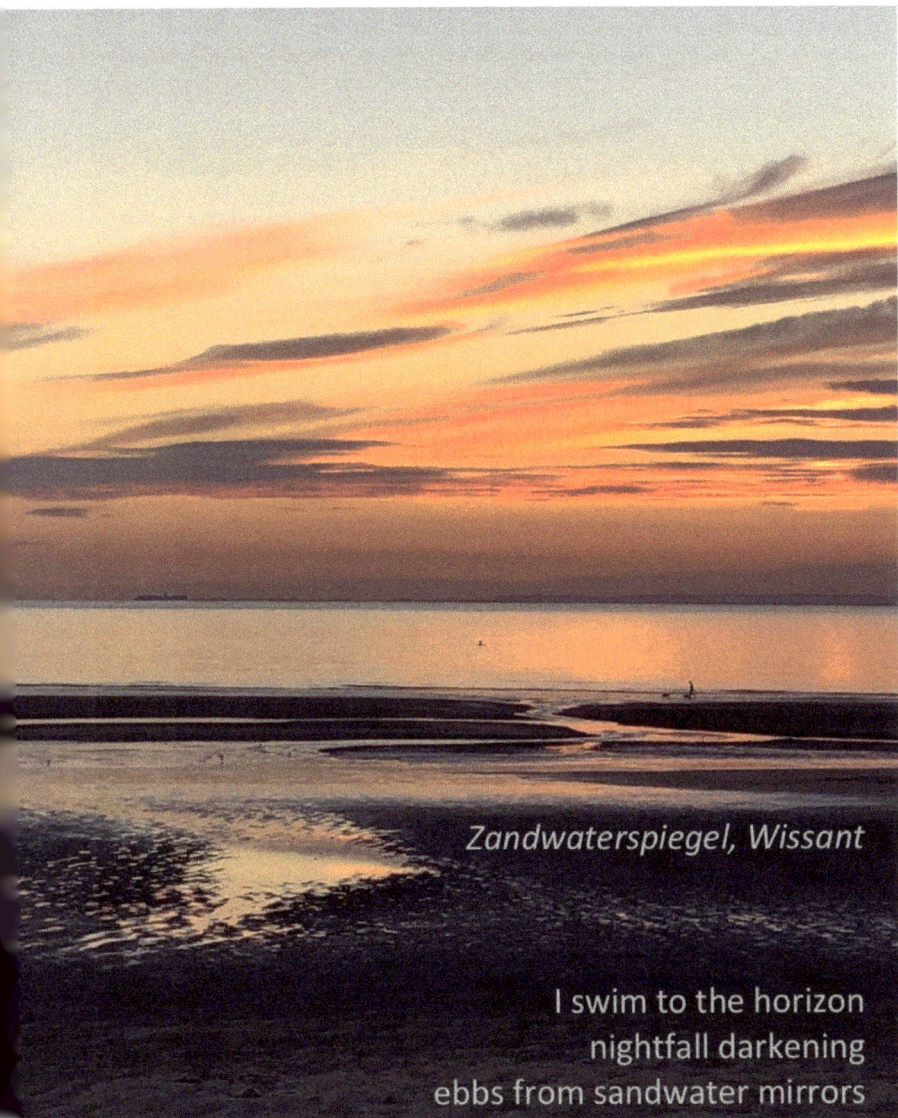

Zandwaterspiegel, Wissant

I swim to the horizon
nightfall darkening
ebbs from sandwater mirrors

In Flight

The Alps were cartoonish sharp
each crinkle precisely hewn
snow held every shade of blue
valleys slung between the peaks
cradled roads that must be going somewhere.

Plastic lunch and a dumb film -
brain and beefcake, off the mark.
As I'd had an early start
I must have slept for a while
when I looked again, I had missed the sea.

Sand whirls, here black, like pools of tar
there red, orange, and turquoise,
pockmarked from giant pumice
ridges throw up stonewall shade.
A deadstraight line that could be a border.

It will be dark when we reach the tropics
I won't see the forest like broccoli
or the pinstriped fields of neon green.
I will state my purpose
and I will have my passport stamped again.

I will watch the city lights
from the backseat of the cab
enjoy the heat, curse the rain
but in this new known unknown town
all is fair to me for I am going home.

Harga
Dido's pyre

Basboosa turned the thousand slights to kindling,
he did not slink away to die in shame.
A human torch that lit
a thousand fires across the Middle East
and singed the fingers of the men in power,
a spark of hope that they might lose their grip.
A beacon to thousands more young men:
a warning their future would be just like his.
Instead they launched a thousand rubber boats
to burn the borders all the way to Italy.

Three thousand years from Dido's pyre:
El-Harga wa lâ al-hogra!

Note: *'El-Harga wa lâ al-hogra!'* literally: 'burning is better than humiliation'.

In Tunisian dialect *harga*, meaning burning and the pain of mourning, has come to denote the dangerous attempts at migration across the Mediterranean by (mainly) young men, prompted by the self-immolation of Mohammed Bouazizi, or Basboosa, in 2011, which sparked the fall of the Ben Ali regime in Tunisia and the so-called 'Arab Spring'.

The Laughing Dove

While bee-eaters snatch a glide
and the woodpecker shrills
and the hooded crow waits
and the swallows chime
and the sunbirds flit,

While hawks hang over the desert
and the chukars race up the cliff
and the hoopoes drill the grit
and the jays heckle
and the bulbuls dive,

While horses wait in cannon-shade
and batons beat on armoured boots
and your face is scarfed
and your eyes are teared
and your wrists are blooded,

While people sleep under the house
and the shield rises
and the shelters open
and the sky flares bright
and the air can't breathe,
the laughing dove is still.

Wind Map

Was it only when
we learnt to fly that our
sights lowered, that we staked our own
earthbound plots bordered with forests
of paper forms to prove who I am, where I grew
up, out grew, who I grew with or away?

                                                     Questions heavy

with deterrent, with repellent, with
hostile environment, that seep toxic
sludge into the daily grind and feed suspicion-laden spores

           Here's a question: Have you ever seen a wind map?

Note: The first part is a Golden Shovel poem after Jeanine Hall Gailey 'The Last Love Poem.'

air murmurates over hard edges over land and sea in swirling waves that could right our list

rock us out of our self-orbit

give us the chance to migrate on a passing trade wind

random gust

when we have flown and floated

drifted and wandered

then, maybe then, when we are becalmed

can we believe our minds' eyes

over a set of TV images?

III. Park Walks

Walk in the Park I

للمزيد من الناس يتحدثون

lub może to lubić

בוקר טוב

екоторые туристы говорят

사람들 이야기

but you know

Warandepark

Six voices curl into the sycamore dome,
blend with the yellow-green light.
Soprano replaces castrato, I think,
from a bench by the curlicued bandstand.
It's empty now; the singers would be
in the narthex, if this were a church.

It's not, of course. Voice four cracks slightly.
Spread men in suits eat sandwiches
their burble buoying the polyphony.
Hiphop from a cheap speaker deepens the bass.
Voice three loses his place,
his neighbour points to the score.

The fountain spurts water two metres high
cooling the formal circle of smoothed stone
prudish nudes, lunchtime bench-meets,
and kids paddling in the green pool.
Bushy corners rustle and joggers lap
between palace and parliament.

The last chord hangs, then dissipates
out from under the sycamore canopy
past the fin de siècle architecture
along the espaliered avenues
around the fountain and its pool, the nudes and the busts
the lunchers, cottagers, paddlers and joggers

until it is swallowed by the traffic
where *Arts* meets *Loi*.

Square Ambiorix

Art nouveau façades glory in sunlight
children swing and slide and squabble, while a
dachshund with a wheeled behind peers up at
pigeons crowning bronze heroes on horseback.
Police pedal past, their helmets cutting
diamond-patterned shade. Behind a listed
townhouse, office juniors watch their week in
washing spin out once more through the cycle.

Across the square, the young man sweeps a drive.
This sun, this land, is cold yet here at least
he can be out in open view, full voice.
But those who count say that the place he fled
is safe. He must go back.
                        There is no room
for him here on this graceful square, its fine
tendrils pulsating his ancestral blood.

Walk in the Park II

Walk in the Park III

zeg, de volgende keer

يتحدث الناس

ona rozmawia przez telefon

it was all on hold

je m'en fous   anyway

gravel mud gravel puddle puddle gravel mud gravel mud gravel puddle puddle
gravel mud gravel puddle puddle gravel mud gravel mud gravel puddle puddle
gravel mud gravel puddle puddle gravel mud gravel puddle puddle puddle
gravel gravel gravel wavulana wanatembea

IV. Vent
Three Mathews Corpus

Four rue

Main fort dent, gout calmer tape
pour par a son tire
tout verse fond a carer tale
four rue loin vent.

Pain rate chose fin roman tort
range tot car bout rape,
rang dent dont roman sort
four rue loin vent.

On tour

Slave tapes us
salve slips sale.

Roman voles sang rot on river:
vague pin, tapir prise, or pet tot?

Coin the mare, pair miner champs
mate verger, miser, nonce.

Grasses assist sage pressing riper chars,
tents tilt, porter devises polar pack -

office report or vent on font?

As Roman As

A found Mathews Corpus

The first French-language fiction book I came across on my bookshelf was Le mystère Henri Pick by David Foenkinos. It opened at random at pages 100-101. The first English-language book I came across in a similar genre was Big Sky by Kate Atkinson. Pages 100-101 in Big Sky were also a double-page spread, so I used these two double pages to find this Mathews Corpus.

Ignoring accents but otherwise keeping strictly to spelling, I identified the words that are written the same and mean something different in English and in French (Mathews Corpus). Each word was recorded in the order of emergence from each text, alternating between the two and starting with Henri Pick, without allowing immediate repetition of the same word.

As Roman As

do son as roman as
as an son a dont
an fit issue zang nine
a tout a
roman are a N
a case lit or roman
a on son a son
on a as a
court or tout
a son a on
dure son tout
son a son
roman son roman.

V. Evitan on Ikenild Street

This found poem play in three scenes was found in The Return of the Native, by Thomas Hardy (Penguin Classics edition, 1999, glossary by Tony Slade).

Each line is the first sentence found in Hardy's text containing each of the terms, in order, from the glossary bar two, the meanings of which are now overshadowed by derogatory current usage.

Given names have been removed and reported speech rendered direct.

Some descriptions are reframed as stage directions.

Cast of Characters

Evitan:	masked
Jane:	an everywoman
John:	an everyman
Chorus:	masked

Masks should, where possible, be made from the text of *The Return of the Native*

Scene:

On and near Ikenild Street.

Action is ad lib by CAST

Scene 1

(<u>JANE</u> and <u>JOHN</u> speak to each other, <u>EVITAN</u>
and <u>CHORUS</u> stand apart)

<u>JANE</u>

She has been stung by an adder!

<u>JOHN</u>

He did not. And there is now no slight on
her name. I was hastening ath'art to tell
you at once, as I saw you were not there.

There was I, straight as a young poplar,
wi' my firelock, and my bagnet, and my
splatterdashes, and my stock sawing my jaws
off, and my accoutrements sheening like the
seven stars.

I am no drinker, as we know, but when the
womenfolk and youngsters have gone home we

can drop down across to the Quiet Woman,
and strike up a ballet in front of the
married folks' door.

JANE

He and your mother were the couple
married just afore we were, and there
stood thy father's cross with arms
stretched out like a great banging
scarecrow.

JOHN

It was a barrow.

JANE

Gorget, gusset, basinet, cuirass,
gauntlet, sleeve, all alike in the view
of these feminine eyes were practicable
spaces whereon to sew scraps of
fluttering colour.

You must not becall me for laughing when you spoke; you mistook when you thought I laughed at you as a foolish man.

(in a liquid tone)

"Well, be dazed if he who do marry the maid won't hae an uncommon picture for his best parlour," said he, placing down the cup of mead at the end of a good pull.

EVITAN

As with Farinelli's singing before the princesses, Sheridan's renowned Begum Speech, and other such examples, the fortunate condition of its being for ever lost to the world invested the deceased's *tour de force* on that memorable afternoon with a cumulative glory which comparative criticism, had that been possible, might considerably have shorn down.

JOHN

"I'm sure when I heard they'd been forbid I felt as glad as if anybody had gied me sixpence," said an earnest voice – that of Olly Dowden, a woman who lived by making heath brooms, or besoms.

The most enduring of all – steady unaltering eyes like planets – signified wood, such as hazel branches, thorn-bundles, and stout billets.

JANE

A bit and a drap wouldn't be amiss now, I reckon.

I was picking black-hearts, and they don't grow nearer.

JOHN

Think what I have gone through to win
her consent; the insult that it is to
any man to have the banns forbidden; the
double insult to a man unlucky enough to
be cursed with sensitiveness, and blue
demons, and heaven knows what, as I am.

JANE

He wore a glazed hat, an ancient boat-
cloak, and shoes; this brass buttons
bearing an anchor upon their face.

JOHN

She had watched the assemblage through
the hole; and seeing that now was the
proper moment to enter, she went from the
'linhay' and boldly pulled the bobbin of
the fuel-house door.

JANE

And now the reddleman has in his turn followed Buonaparte to the land of worn-out bogeys, and his place is filled by modern inventions.

But in the year four 'twas said there wasn't a finer figure in the whole South Wessex than I, as I looked when dashing past the shop-winders with the rest of our company on the day we ran out o' Budmouth because it was thoughted that Boney had landed round the point.

JOHN

This bossy projection of earth above its natural level occupied the loftiest ground of the loneliest height that the heath contained.

JANE

The roof and chimney of his caravan showed beyond the tracery and tangles of the brake.

Its condition is recorded therein as that of heathy, furzy, briary wilderness – 'Bruaria'

JOHN

I've made but a bruckle hit, I'm afeared.

EVITAN

No reply was returned by his companion, since none could be given; and when the man left, a few minutes later another had passed from the dullness of sorrow to the fluctuation of carking incertitude.

JOHN

Your sentiment on the wisdom of *Carpe Diem* does not impress me to-day.

JANE

"It must be here," said the voice by her side, and blushingly looking up, she saw him removing his casque to kiss her.

JOHN

Her grandfather returned, and was busily engaged in pouring some gallons of newly-arrived rum into the square bottles of his square cellaret.

Smiling champaigns of flowers and fruit hardly do this, for they are permanently harmonious only with an existence of better reputation as to its issues than the present.

JANE

At christenings, folk will even smuggle in a reel or two, if 'tis no further on than the first or second chiel.

JOHN

Upon my soul, I shall be chokt

(he extracts a feather from his mouth,
finds several others flowing on the mug
as it was handed round).

'tis cleft-wood, that's what 'tis.

EVITAN

The breeze that blew around his mouth in
that walk carried off in them the accents
of a commination.

JANE

Except the daughter of one of the
cotters, who was their servant, and a
lad who worked in the garden and stable,
scarcely anyone but themselves ever
entered the house.

When I think of you and your new crotchets

(with emphasis)

I naturally don't feel as comfortable as I did a twelvemonth ago.

CHORUS

Gorget, gusset, basinet, cuirass, gauntlet, sleeve, all alike in the view of these feminine eyes were practicable spaces whereon to sew scraps of fluttering colour.

JOHN

Well, this is a bad night altogether for them that have done well in their time, and if I were ever such a dab at the hautboy or tenor-viol I shouldn't have the heart to play tunes upon 'em now.

JANE

A certain well-to-do air about the man suggested that he was not poor for his degree.

JOHN

But the deuce a bit would they sit down.

JANE

I am going to play dibs afore supper, and we go to supper at six o'clock, because father comes home.

A sight of times better to be selling diments than nobbling about here.

JOHN

To save my soul I couldn't help laughing when I saw en, though all the time I was as hot as dogdays, what with the marrying, and what with the women hanging to me, and what with Jack Changley and

a lot more chaps grinning at me though
church window.

EVITAN

The gaunt oak-cased clock, with the
picture of the Ascension on the door-
panel and the Miraculous Draught of
Fishes on the base; his grandmother's
corner-cupboard with the glass-door,
through which the spotted china was
visible; the dumb-waiter; the wooden
teatrays; the hanging fountain with the
brass tap - wither would these venerable
articles have to be banished?

JOHN

Ear-drops and rings by hatfuls; gold
platters; chains enough to hold an ox,
all washed in gold.

JANE

Once when I went up to Throope Great Pond
to catch effets I seed myself looking up
at myself and I was frightened and jumped
back like anything!

A Saturday afternoon in November was
approaching the time of twilight, and
the vast tract of enclosed wild known as
Egdon Heath embrowned itself moment by
moment.

JOHN

A hopfrog have jumped into the pond, I
saw 'en.

EVITAN

Occasionally she came to a spot where
independent worlds of ephemerons were
passing their time in mad carousal, some

in the air, some on the hot ground and vegetation, some in the tepid and stringy water of a nearly-dried pool.

He preaching to the Egdon eremites that they might rise to a serene comprehensiveness without going through the process of enriching themselves not unlike arguing to ancient Chaldeans that in ascending from earth to the pure empyrean it was not necessary to pass first into the intervening heaven of ether.

JANE

Well, what a fess little bonfire that was is, out by Cap'n Drew's!

JOHN

The wind rasped and scraped at the corners of the house, and filliped the eaves-droppings like peas against the panes.

"Money won't do it," he said, brushing the iron head of the fire-dog with the hollow of his hand.

CHORUS

There was I, straight as a young poplar, wi' my firelock, and my bagnet, and my splatterdashes, and my stock sawing my jaws off, and my accoutrements sheening like the seven stars.

JANE

The smoke went up from an Etna of turf in front of him, played around the notches of the chimney-crook, struck against the salt-box and got lost among the flitches.

                         JOHN

In a moment, an open fly was driven past,
in which they sat, and a grand relative
of his who had come from Budmouth for the
occasion.

                         JANE

Beds be dear to fokes that don't keep
geese, baint they?

                         JOHN

And what ghastly gallicrow might the poor
fellow have been like?

                         JANE

That's my age by baptism, because that's
put down in the great book of the
judgment-day that they keep down in the
church vestry; but mother told me I was
born some time afore I was christened.

CHORUS

Gorget, gusset, basinet, cuirass, gauntlet, sleeve, all alike in the view of these feminine eyes were practicable spaces whereon to sew scraps of fluttering colour.

EVITAN

He was a somewhat solemn young fellow, and carried the hook and leather gloves of a furze-cutter, his legs, by reason of that occupation, being sheathed in bulging leggings as stiff as the Philistine's greaves of brass.

JOHN

The guisers themselves, though inwardly regretting this confusion of persons, could not afford to offend those by whose assistance they so largely profited, and the innovations were allowed to stand.

CHORUS

Gorget, gusset, basinet, cuirass, gauntlet, sleeve, all alike in the view of these feminine eyes were practicable spaces whereon to sew scraps of fluttering colour.

The gaunt oak-cased clock, with the picture of the Ascension on the door-panel and the Miraculous Draught of Fishes on the base; his grandmother's corner-cupboard with the glass-door, through which the spotted china was visible; the dumb-waiter; the wooden teatrays; the hanging fountain with the brass tap – wither would these venerable articles have to be banished?

JOHN

A harrowing old man

(despondingly)

JANE

Then she whose stupor of grief had been
thrust off awhile by frantic action,
applied a bottle of hartshorn to his
nostrils, having tried it in vain upon
the other two.

JOHN

I was a-forced to go back to Lower
Mistover to-night, and he asked me to
leave this here on my way; but, faith,
I put it in the lining of my hat, and
thought no more about it till I got back
and was hasping my gate before going to
bed.

JANE

Well, this is a bad night altogether for
them that have done well in their time,
and if I were ever such a dab at the
hautboy or tenor-viol I shouldn't have
the heart to play tunes upon 'em now.

JOHN

At the end of a minute a dull splashing
reverberated from the bottom of the well;
the helical twist he had imparted to the
rope had reached the grapnel below.

JANE

Well if you don't mind, we'll have beaker,
and pass 'en round: 'tis better than
heling it out in dribbles.

Is this your cherishing - to put me into
a hut like this, and keep me like the
wife of a hind?

EVITAN

While he was closing the little horn door a figure slowly rose from behind a neighbouring bush and came forward into the lantern light.

Egdon Heath is a bad place to get lost in, and the winds to huffle queerer to-night than ever I heard 'em afore.

JANE

But even that might be overcome by time and patience, so as to let a few grey hairs show themselves in the hussy's head.

JOHN

This was large, and in addition to its proper recess, contained within its jambs, like many on Egdon, a reclining seat, so that a person might sit there absolutely

unobserved, provided there was no fire
to light him up, as was the case now and
throughout the summer.

JANE

Jown it, I'm up for anything!

I'm as dry as a kex with biding up here
in the wind, and I haven't seen the
colour of drink since nammet-time to-day.

JOHN

And 'tis on the knap afore the old
captain's house at Mistover.

JANE

I'd sooner go without a drink at Lammas-
tide than be a man of no moon.

(in the same shattered recitative)

EVITAN

Then follows the length and breadth in
leagues; and, though some uncertainty
exists to the exact extent of this
ancient lineal measure, it appears from
the figures that the area of Egdon
down to the present day has but little
diminished.

JANE

I'll crack thy numskull for thee, you
mandy chap

    (as she helplessly danced round with
    him)

her feet playing like drumsticks among
the sparks.

'Tis very nonsense of an old man to
prattle so when life and death's in
mangling.

JOHN

Ah, well I can mind when I was married
how I saw thy father's mark staring me in
the face as I went to put down my name.

EVITAN

A mart extensive enough for the purpose
existed some miles beyond the spot chosen
for his residence, and there he resolved
to pass the coming night.

JANE

Maul down to the victuals from the
corner-cupboard if thou canst reach,
man;' and I'll draw a drop of summat to
wet it with.

JOHN

You know what you forbade me at the
maypoling, miss

(murmured)

without looking at her and still stroking
the fire-dog's head.

We were wondering what could keep you
home here mollyhorning about when you
have made such a worldwide name for
yourself in the nick-nack trade - now,
that's the truth o't.

JANE

Lord's sake, I thought, whatever fiery
mommet is this come to trouble us?

JOHN

Ay, when I think what she'll say to me
now without a mossel of red in her face,
it do seem strange that 'a wouldn't say
such a little thing then….

CHORUS

I'm as dry as a kex with biding up here in the wind, and I haven't seen the colour of drink since nammet-time to-day

JOHN

Really all the soldiering and smartness in the world in the father seems to count for nothing in forming the nater of the son.

They'd look very natty, arm-in-crook together, and their best clothes on, whether or no, if he's at all the well-favoured fellow he used to be.

CHORUS

A sight of times better to be selling
diments than nobbling about here.

EVITAN

As he watched the dead flat of scenery
overpowered him, though he was fully
alive to the beauty of that untarnished
early green summer which was worn for the
nonce by the poorest blade.

CHORUS

I'll crack thy numskull for thee, you
mandy chap

    (as they helplessly danced round
    with him)

her feet playing like drumsticks among
the sparks.

JANE

You see, after kicking up such a
nunnywatch and forbidding the banns
'twould have made her seem foolish-like to
have a banging wedding in the same parish
all as if she'd never gainsaid it all.

Have you seen a ooser?

JOHN

The air became quite still; the flag
above the waggon which held the musicians
clung to the pole, and the players
appeared only in outline against the sky;
except when the circular mouths of the
trombone, ophicleide, and French horn
gleamed out like huge eyes from the shade
of their figures.

EVITAN

The young man learnt with added surprise that the date at which he might expect to resume his labours was as uncertain as ever, his eyes being in that peculiar state which, though affording him sight enough for walking about, would not admit of their being strained upon any definite object without incurring the risk of reproducing ophthalmia in its acute form.

JANE

It should be in day by outstep, ill-accounted places like this!

JOHN

He was standing with his back to the fireplace, smoking a cigar; and the promoter of the raffle, a packman from a distant town, was expatiating upon the value of the fabric as material for a summer dress.

He looked wistfully to the top of the bank at the woman who stood there, and his teeth, which were quite unimpaired, showed like parian from his parted lips.

It had as many ramifications as the Cretan labyrinth, as many fluctuations as the Northern Lights, as much colour as a parterre in June, was as crowded with figures as a coronation.

JANE

She was a woman noisily constructed: in addition to her enclosing framework of whalebone and lath, she wore pattens summer and winter, in wet weather and in dry, to preserve her boots from wear; and when he began to jump about with her, the clicking of the pattens, the creaking of the stays, and her screams of surprise, formed a very audible concert.

She was perforce content.

She was thus convinced that the reddleman was a mere *pis aller* in her mind, one, moveover who had not been informed of his promotion to that lowly standing.

JOHN

Them that know Egdon best have been pixy-led here at times.

How could this be otherwise, in the days of square fields, plashed hedges, and meadows watered on a plan so rectangular that on a fine day they look like silver gridirons?

JANE

I wouldn't live with him a week, so
playward as he is, if I could get away

EVITAN

A bleeding about the poll on Sunday
afternoons was amply accounted for by the
explanation, 'I have had my hair cut, you
know'

JOHN

It was herself, occupied in preparing
a posset for her little boy, who, often
ailing, was now seriously unwell.

JANE

The turf-cutter seized her and, somewhat
more gently, poussetted with her likewise.

JOHN

And how is your poor purblind husband?

JANE

The house was encrusted with heavy thatchings, which dropped between the upper windows; the front, upon which the moonbeams directly played, had originally been white; but a huge pyracanth now darkened the greater portion.

There is a quag between us and that light, and you will walk into it up to your neck unless I take you round

EVITAN

He walked restlessly about the untenanted rooms, stopping strange noises in windows and doors by jamming splinters of wood into the casements and crevices, and pressing together the lead-work of the quarries where it had become loosened from the glass.

Not that this couple be in want of one, but 'twas well to show 'em a bit of friendliness at this great racketing vagary of their lives.

JOHN

The reddleman looked grim, threw a raffle of aces, and pocketed the stakes.

'Tis said I be only the rames of a man, and no good in the world at all; and I suppose that's the cause o't.

EVITAN

A small apple-tree, of the sort called Ratheripe grew just inside the gate, the only one which thrived in the garden, by reason of the lightness of the soil; and among the fallen apples on the ground beneath were wasps rolling drunk with the juice, or creeping about the little caves

in each fruit which they had eaten out
before stupefied by its sweetness.

JANE

The fire soon revealed itself to be lit,
not on the level ground, but on a salient
corner or redan of earth, at the junction
of the two converging bank fences.

JOHN

A Rencounter by the Pool.

She drew from the small willow reticule
that she carried in her hand an old-
fashioned china teacup without a handle;
it was one of half-a-dozen of the same
sort lying in the reticule, which she had
preserved ever since her childhood, and
had brought with her to-day as a small
present for them.

JANE

And then, when they got to the church-
door he'd throw down the clarinet, mount
the gallery, snatch up the bass-viol,
and rozum away as if he'd never played
anything but a bass-viol.

EVITAN

Who are you? he asked, discerning by the
candlelight an obscure rubicundity of
person in his companion.

JOHN

So perhaps I shall rub on?

JANE

Now a few russets.

JOHN

He used to like them almost as well as
ribstones.

JANE

And even as 'tis we all took a little scammish beside him.

They say he can talk French as fast as a maid can eat blackberries; and if so, depend upon it we who have stayed at home shall seem no more than scroff in this eyes.

EVITAN

With his stick in his hand he began to jig a private minuet, a bunch of copper seals shining and swinging like a pendulum from under his waistcoat: he also began to sing, in the voice of a bee up a flue.

Every now and then a long low note from the serpent, which was the chief wind instrument played at these times,

advanced further into the heath than the
thin treble part, and reached their ears
alone; and next a more than usually loud
tread from a dancer would come the same
way.

JOHN

At the other side of the chimney stood
the settle, which is the necessary
supplement to a fire so open that nothing
less than a strong breeze will carry up
the smoke.

He had got one pot of the bones, and
was going to bring 'em home - real
skellington bones - but 'twas ordered
otherwise.

JANE

What does it mean - it is not skimmity-
riding, I hope?

    (frightened)

JOHN

'Twill please the young wife, and that's
what I should like to do, for many's the
skinful I've had at her hands when she
lived with her aunt at Blooms-End.

At that time women used to run for smocks
and gown-pieces at Greenhill Fair, and
my wife that is now, being a long-legged
slittering maid hardly husband-high, went
with the rest of the maidens, for 'a was
a good runner afore she got so heavy.

I did not know there had ever been
anything between you till lately; and,
faith, I should have been hot and strong
against it if I had known; but it seems
that there was some sniffing between ye,
why the deuce didn't you stick to him?

JANE

What snipe you were in that matter!

You are aware that I have a little box full of spade-guineas, which your uncle put into my hands to divide between yourself and him whenever I chose.

CHORUS

There was I, straight as a young poplar, wi' my firelock, and my bagnet, and my splatterdashes, and my stock sawing my jaws off, and my accoutrements sheening like the seven stars.

EVITAN

With a speäker, or stake, he tossed the outlying scraps of fuel into the conflagration, looking at the midst of the pile, occasionally lifting his eyes to measure the height of the flame, or to follow the great sparks which rose with it and sailed away into darkness.

JANE

When he drew nearer, he perceived it to be a spring van, ordinary in shape, but singular in colour, this being a lurid red.

JOHN

One evening when he was thus standing in the garden, abstractedly spudding up a weed with his stich, a bony figure turned the corner of the house and came up to him.

JANE

A fair stave, but I am afeared 'tis too much for the mouldy weasand of such a old man as you.

CHORUS

There was I, straight as a young poplar, wi' my firelock, and my bagnet, and my splatterdashes, and my stock sawing my jaws off, and my accoutrements sheening like the seven stars.

JANE

But the next moment a strawmote would have knocked me down, for I called to mind that if thy father and mother had had high words once, they'd been at it twenty times since they'd been man and wife, and I saw myself as the next poor stunpoll to get into the same mess....

CHORUS

But the next moment a strawmote would have knocked me down, for I called to mind that if thy father and mother had had high words once, they'd been at it twenty times since they'd been man and wife, and I saw myself as the next poor stunpoll to get into the same mess….

JOHN
Thirty-one last, tatie-digging, mister.

JANE
A young woman with a home must be a fool to tear her smock for a man like that.

EVITAN
Only one sound rose above this din of weather, and that was the roaring of a ten-hatch weir a few yards further on, where the road approached the river which formed the boundary of the heath in this direction.

JOHN
Dostn't wish th' wast three sixes again, as you was when you first learnt to sing?

JANE

'Tis well to call the neighbours together
and have a good racket once now and then;
and it may as well be when there's a
wedding as at tide-times.

JOHN

Come under my tilt and let me tie it up.

JANE

I ha'n't been there to-year and now the
winter is a-coming on I won't say I
shall.

EVITAN

With her dropping out of sight on the
right side a new-comer, bearing a burden,
protruded into the sky on the left side,
ascended the tumulus, and deposited the
burden on the top.

Turbaria Bruaria - the right of cutting
heath-turf - occurs in charters relating
to the district.

To see the heathmen in their Sunday
condition, that is, with their hands in
their pockets, their boots newly oiled,
and not laced (a particularly Sunday
sign), walking leisurely among the turves
.. they had cut down during the week, and
kicking them critically as if their use
were unknown, was a fearful heaviness to
her.

JOHN

Only he is twanky because 'tisn't a boy -
that's what they say in the kitchen.

EVITAN

If, in passing under one of the Egdon
banks, any of its thick skeins were

caught, as they sometimes were, by a
prickly tuft of the large Ulex Europæus
- which will act as a sort of hairbrush
- she would go back a few steps, and pass
against it a second time.

JOHN

There was no middle distance in her
perspective: romantic collections of sunny
afternoons on an esplanade, with military
bands, officers and gallants around,
stood like gilded unicals upon the dark
tablet of surrounding Egdon.

EVITAN

This unweeting manner of performance
is the true ring by which, in this
refurbishing age, a fossilized
survival may be known from a spurious
reproduction.

JANE

And there were few in these parts that
were up-sides with him.

A man should be only partially before his
time: to be completely to the vanward in
aspirations is fatal to fame.

JOHN

Yes, this morning at six o'clock they
went up the country to do the job, and
neither vell nor mark have been seen
of 'em since, though I reckon that this
afternoon has brought 'em home again, man
and woman – wife, that is.

In many portions of its course it
overlaid and old vicinal way, which
branched from the great Western road of
the Romans, the Via Iceniana, or Ikenild
Street.

JANE

My ancles were all in a fever afore, from walking through that prickly furze, and now you must make 'em worse with these vlankers!

CHORUS

A fair stave, but I am afeared 'tis too much for the mouldy weasand of such a old man as you.

EVITAN

Half-a-dozen able-bodied men were standing in a line from the well-mouth, holding a rope which passed over the well-roller into the depths below.

JOHN

Wethers must live their time as well as other sheep, poor soul.

CHORUS

She was a woman noisily constructed: in addition to her enclosing framework of whalebone and lath, she wore pattens summer and winter, in wet weather and in dry, to preserve her boots from wear; and when he began to jump about with her, the clicking of the pattens, the creaking of the stays, and her screams of surprise, formed a very audible concert.

EVITAN

In her anxiety to get out of the direct
view of the house she had diverged
from the straightest path homeward,
and while looking about to regain it
she came across a little boy gathering
whortleberries in a hollow.

JANE

He is a man who notices the looks of women, and you could twist him to your will like withywind, if you only had the mind.

JOHN

And what a zany an old chap must be, to light a bonfire when there's no youngsters to please.

(CAST leave the stage)

Scene 2

CHORUS

(CHORUS enter. CHORUS wear strips of cloth carrying the lines of Scene 1 very loosely stitched to their clothing. They dance in the manner of the English country dances that figure in *The Return of the Native*, or similar. The strips fall to the ground. The dance ends when all the strips are on the ground.)

(CHORUS remain on stage, still.)

Scene 3

(EVITAN, JANE, JOHN enter. Starting from the closest point to the audience and working clockwise, EVITAN, JANE and JOHN each read in order of discovery, a line of text.)

(When they reach the final line of text, which should be centre stage, close to audience, EVITAN straightens the final line out on the ground in front of the CAST. ALL CAST read the final line.)

THE END

THOMAS HARDY

The Return of the Native

VI. November

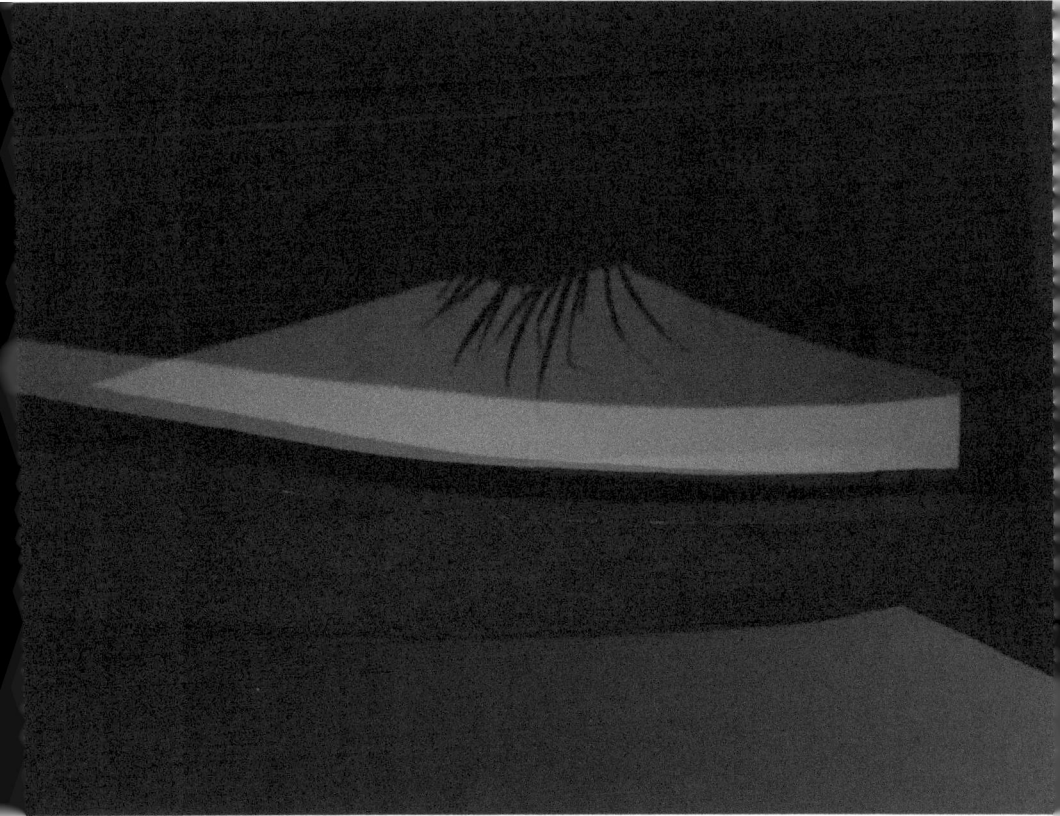

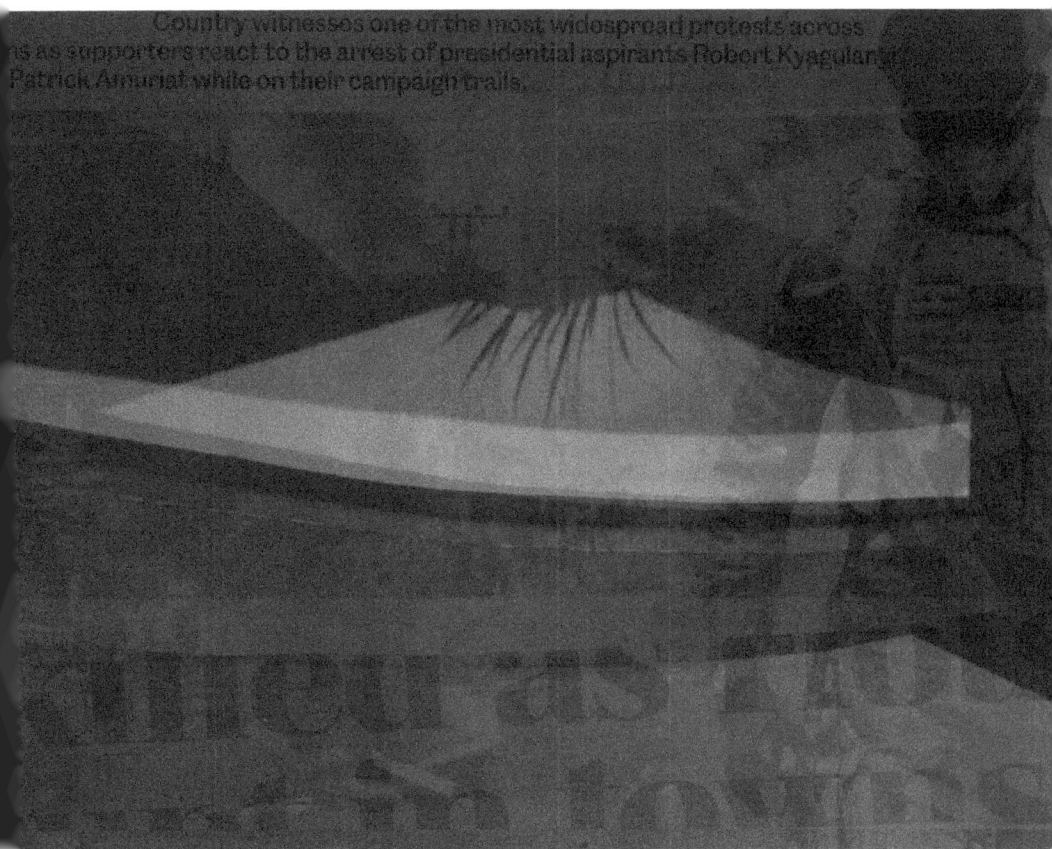

Country witnesses one of the most widespread protests across [...]ns as supporters react to the arrest of presidential aspirants Robert Kyagulan[...] Patrick Amuriat while on their campaign trails.

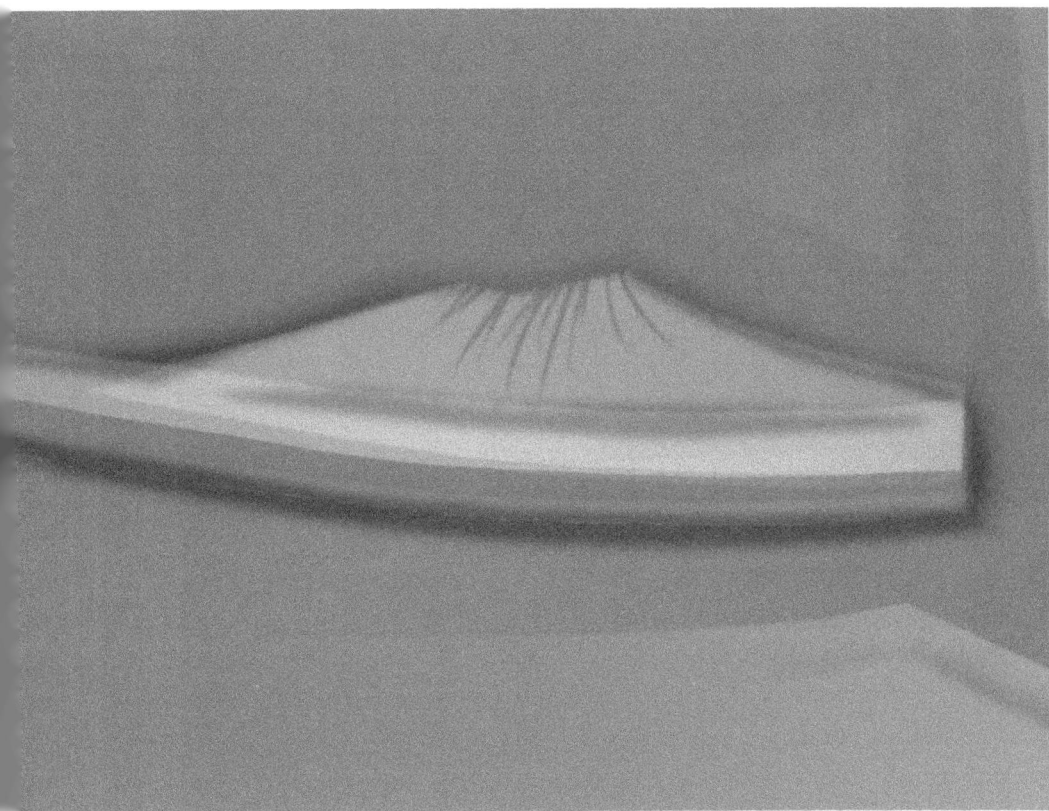

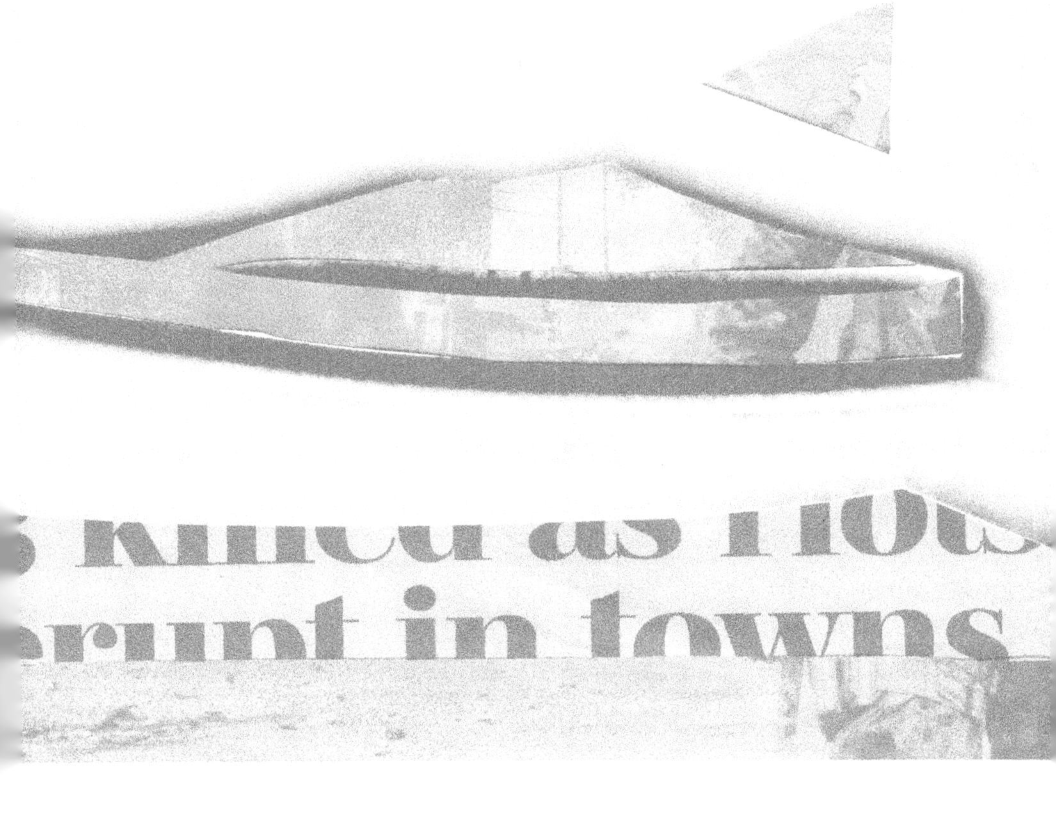
in towns

VII. H, Darkly

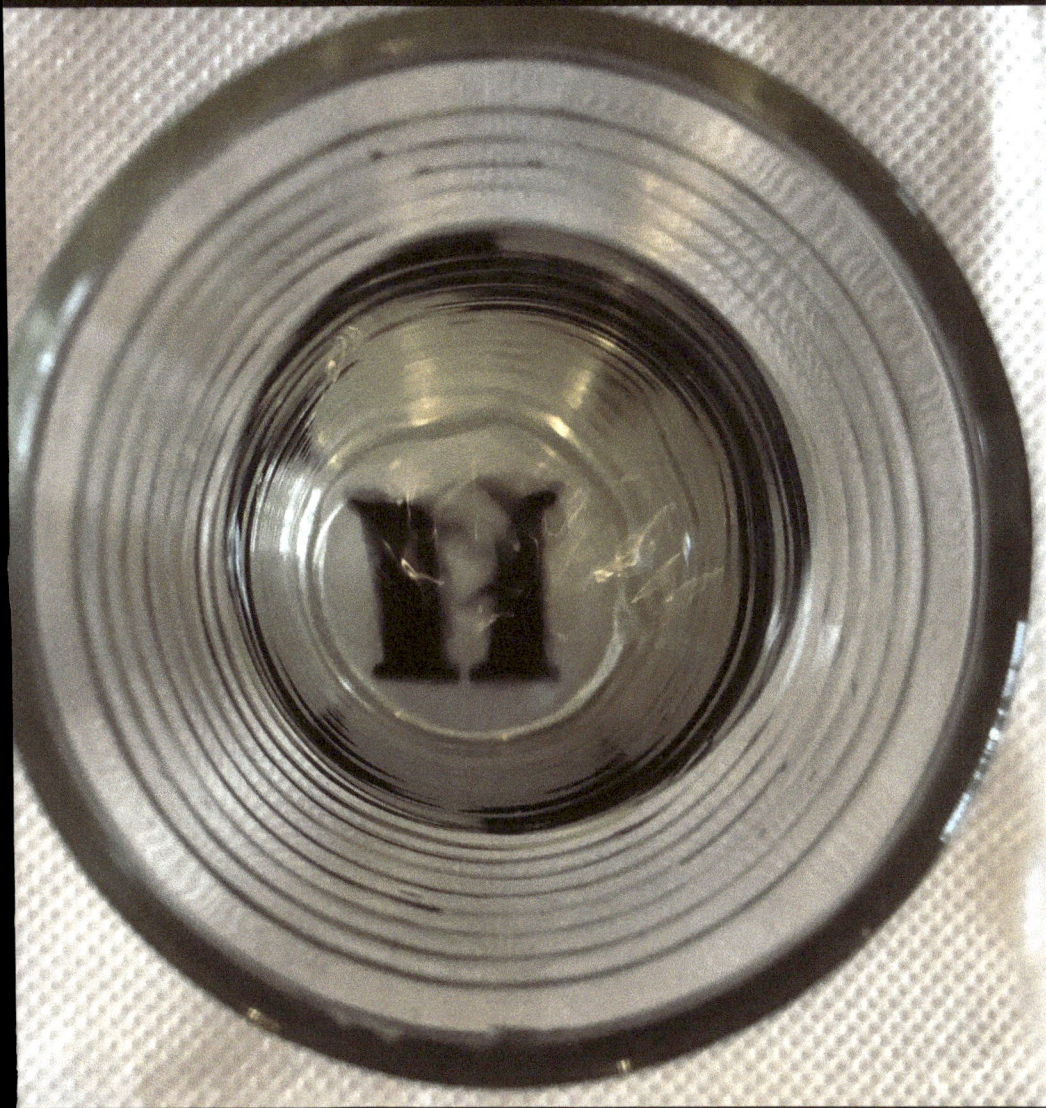

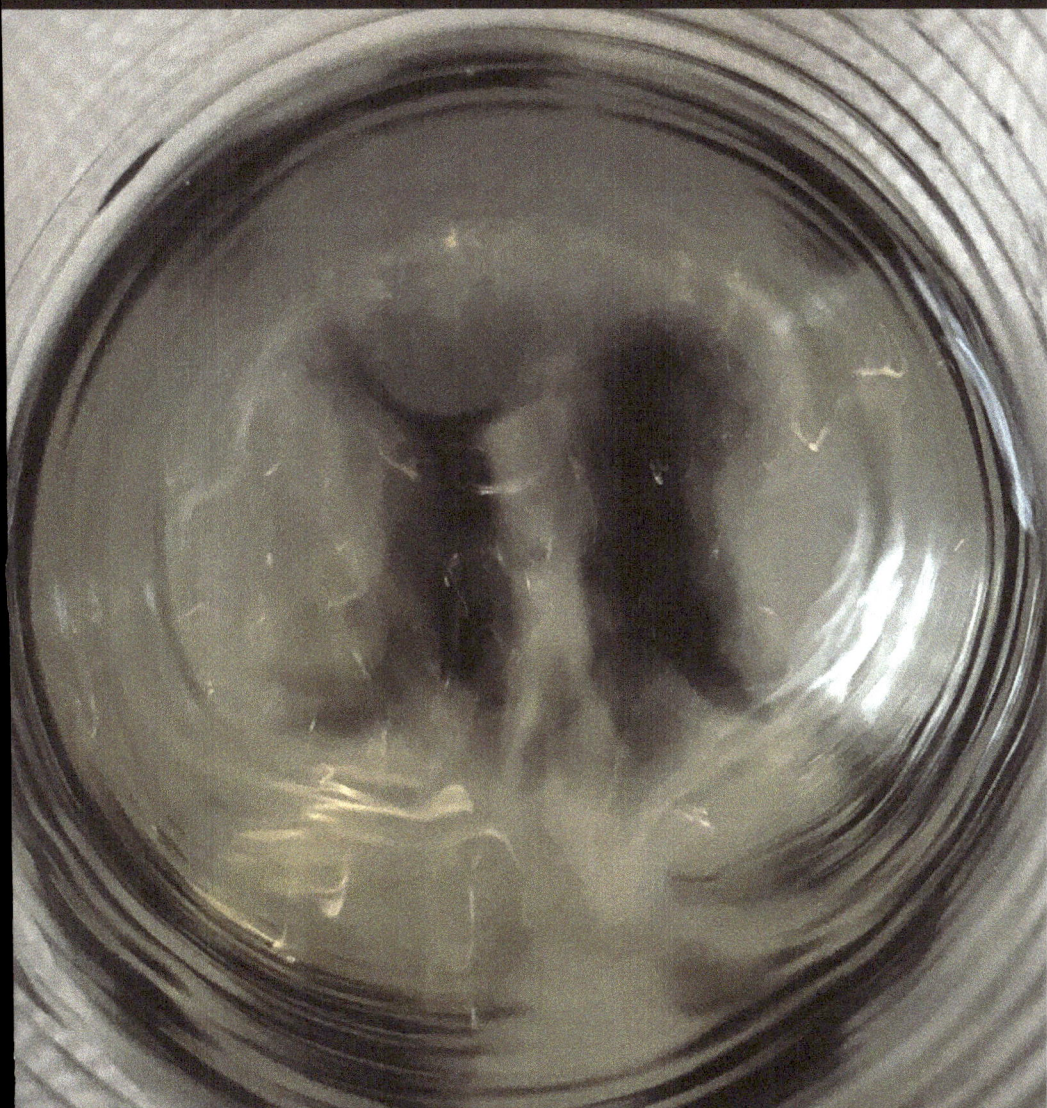

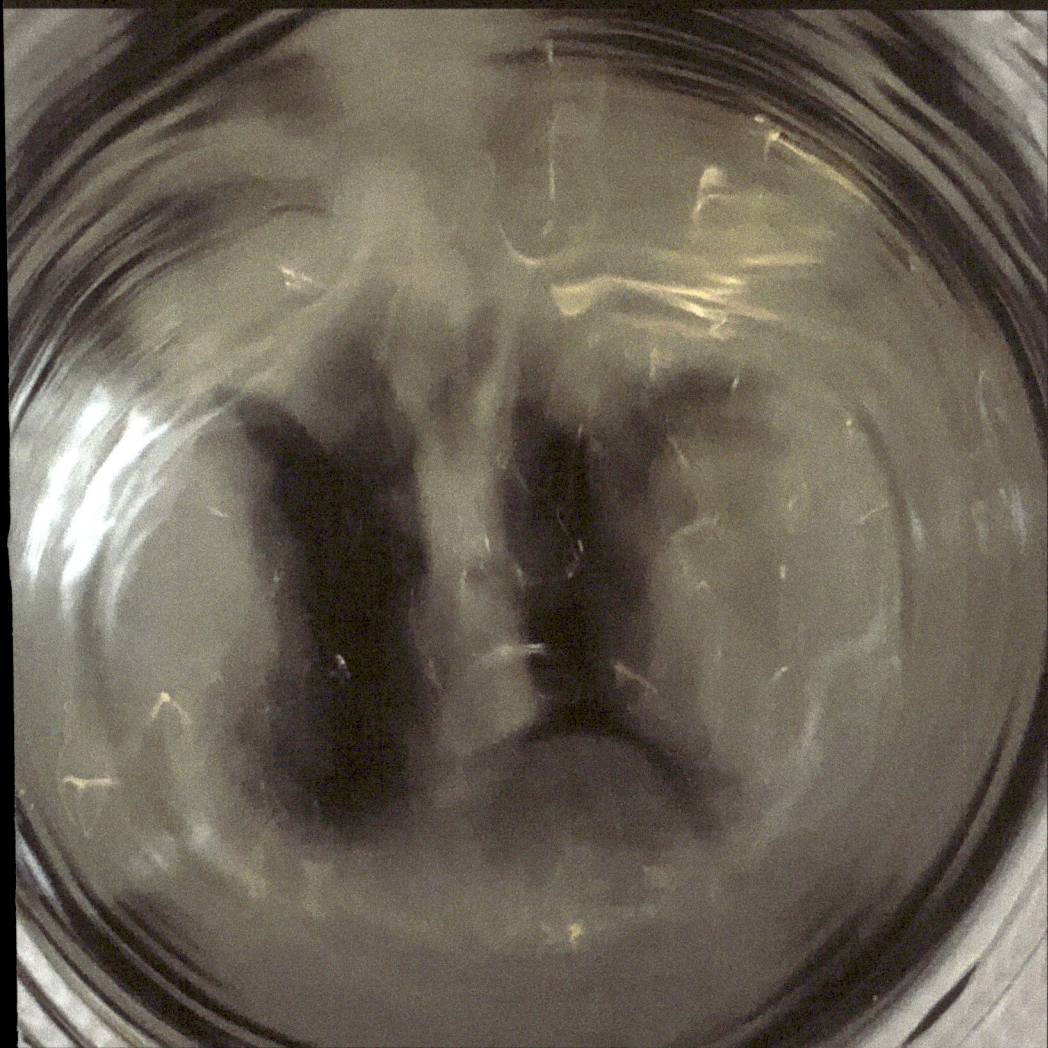

Acknowledgements

This book – and many of the poems in it – would have stayed in the ether without the inspiration, encouragement and expert eye of SJ Fowler and the amazing PoPoGrou community of poets he catalyses. I am so grateful to be part of it. Thank you all – particularly Susie Campbell and Sylee Gore – for your brilliance and generosity.

A huge thank you to my daughter Charlotte Horemans for her collaboration on the Evitan dance and in The Way We Live Now I and for her support and inspiration.

And thanks too of course to Emma Tait, Arwa Nadeem, Miranda Gonzalez Farrington, Sophie Boddington, Vanshika Parmar, and Zoe Bott at Kingston University Press.

Sources and Inspirations

I. Illustrations and Interruptions

www.ingramcontent.com/pod-product-compliance
Lightning Source LLC
LaVergne TN
LVHW010304070426
835508LV00026B/3431